THE PHONEY PHANTOM GOPHER

Clive Gifford

Illustrated by Janet Samuel

Pheasant Field, with its stream and trees, was a pleasant place to see.
Pheasants hid in thorny bushes and thrushes nested in the trees.
Swans swam through Swallow Stream, which stretched across the land.
And Thistle Thicket contained strawberry bushes, which was grand.

One day, humans arrived
and the thrushes f l e w away.
The rumble of engines made
the swans swim off.

Pheasant Field had been
bought by a builder, Mr Heath.
His swarm of workers and
machines stripped the earth.

Only some gophers stayed
in their burrows beneath.
And soon, even they would
have to pack and leave.

2

Can you draw a line between the pairs of words which rhyme?

path

birth

pheasant

forth

phone

beneath

stray

bath

earth

mouth

south

pleasant

north

sway

teeth

throne

The gophers were led by the head gopher, called **BIG** Bill.
He was three times the size of the smallest gopher, called Phil.

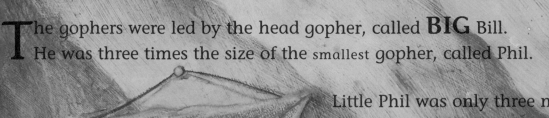

Little Phil was only three months old
when he learned the alphabet.
Now he kept lots of books
in his home beneath Thistle Thicket.

Phil didn't want to leave Pheasant Field's land.
He told his friend, Theo, about his great plan.

"Some people froth at the mouth when they see gophers.
I read it in a book. The illness is called gopher phobia.
I think if we could make a huge phoney phantom gopher,
it might scare Mr Heath into leaving Pheasant Field."

4

Add ph, th or f to each set of letters to make the word the clue describes.

_____ ick – the opposite of thin

_____ ief – someone who steals

_____ ield – an area of grass or farmland

_____ oney – something or someone that is a fake

_____ irsty – really wanting and needing a drink

_____ antom – another word for ghost or something spooky

_____ ree – not costing anything or to let something go

_____ imble – the little cup people put on a
finger when sewing

Phil and Theo worked on the plan throughout the night.
Phil thought up some words and phrases to write.
Thirteen gophers made a pyramid and were covered in a sheet.

On top of their backs stood Theo, baring his teeth.
Phil took a photo of the phoney phantom gopher
just before...
the thirteen gophers fell to the floor. **Thud!**

Theo groaned, "Hope your
phantom gopher plan works, Phil."
"My head is thumping
like thunder
from falling over!"

Phil printed his words and the photo in a pamphlet,
then left the pamphlets in the field. His plan was now set.

Here is an early version of Phil's pamphlet. There are ten spelling mistakes. Can you find all the mistakes and make the corrections?

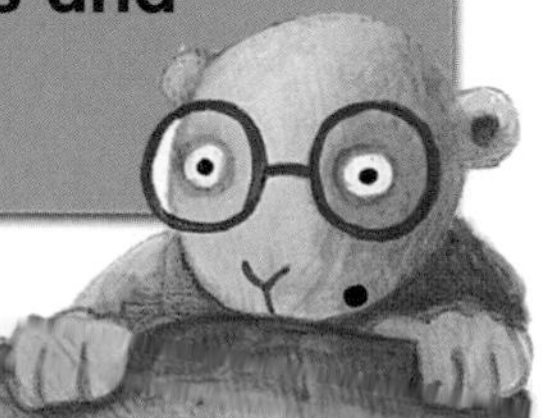

Bewear the fantom of Feasant Field.

Please leaf the feeled to the gophers – or else.

Their will be funder and rane for free years.

When the phantom gofer rises, bad men will fall.

"What's this strange pamphlet?" said head workman, Seth.

Phil hid by Thistle Thicket and held his breath.

Seth read the pamphlet and then chuckled with mirth. "A phantom gopher… gopher phobia… just **myths**, that's all!"

WHEN THE PHANTOM GOPHER RISES, BAD MEN WILL FALL!

Phil watched the other workmen swear and curse and tear up their pamphlets or chuckle with mirth.

It was the truth. Phil thought he might cry. Mr Heath's workmen had seen through his lies. He went back to his burrow – he needed to hide.

Remove a letter from each of the following words to make a new word. Use the clues to help you.

thrash – a slang word for rubbish _____ _____

sweat – another word for a chair or bench _____

booth – a type of footwear _____

thorn – an object that can make a beeping sound _____

swings – birds have two of these _____ _____

forth – a type of castle _____

health – a type of moor or common _____

strip – another word for journey _____

Thirty miles away,
Mr Heath was in his big home.
He thought about his wealth
and picked up the phone.
He rang the workmen in Pheasant Field,
gnashing his teeth.

"When are you thick thugs going to turn that field into streets?"

"Things have been tough, boss," moaned Seth.
"I have three men off with a strange gopher illness."

Mr Heath roared, "The truth is that gopher phobia's a myth.
It's all lies and nonsense. It's a phoney illness.
First, you said the third of the month, then the fifth, then the eighth.
Turn that field into streets **NOW**, or you'll regret being late!"

10

Here is a map of Pheasant Field. The route from the strawberry bushes to the trees with the thrushes' nests is drawn in a dotted line. Can you write six sentences of instructions using the words **North**, **South**, **East** and **West** to describe the route to someone? Use the compass to help you.

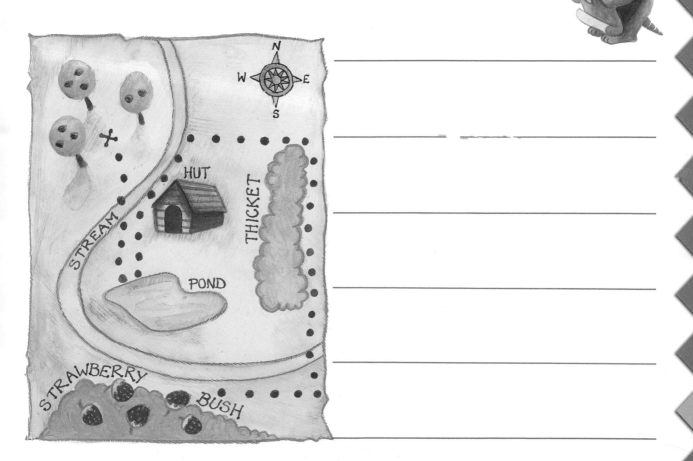

_____

_____

_____

_____

_____

_____

11

Mr Heath's machines swarmed in past Swallow Stream.
The earth around Thistle Thicket was dug up by one machine.
A digger thrashed through Phil's burrow, to his alarm.

It dug close to Phil, and he feared he would come to harm.
Phil's little mouth and teeth were not good for tunnelling work
but now he dug for all he was worth.
He dug for his life!

The other gophers were on the far side of Pheasant Field.
They were packing their things and getting ready to leave.

"Where's Phil?" they shouted.
"Those filthy machines are moving in!"

The head gopher cried,
"Gophers, get busy burrowing!"

Can you find these eight words in the grid below? The hidden words run up, down and across the grid.

swamp   teeth   sweet   threat

photo   that   stop   strip

C	S	T	O	P
S	W	A	M	P
T	E	E	T	H
R	E	R	F	O
I	T	H	A	T
P	Q	T	G	O

The gophers ran through their tunnels from end to end.
They searched the length and breadth for their missing friend.
They dug a thousand new tunnels and looked round every bend.

At three in the morning, the gophers heard Big Bill.
"Hurrah! Great triumph, I have found little Phil!"

Phil was tired and filthy,
but also hungry and thirsty.
The gophers fed him strawberries
and thimbles full of herb tea.

The head gopher's wife, Ruth,
stroked his head.
"There, there, little Phil,
you did try your best.
We'll be leaving soon,
but there's time for a bath and a rest."

14

Add either **str** or **sw** to the start of each of these groups of letters to form a word. One set of letters can use both.

_____ amp

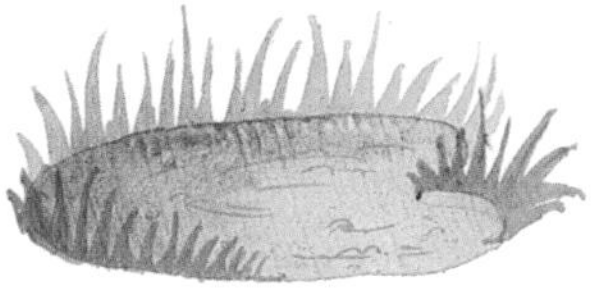

_____ ide

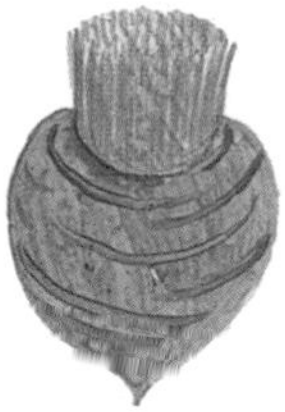

_____ ede

_____ oke

_____ oop

_____ arm

_____ aight

_____ ap

_____ ap

The next day, the diggers thundered past Swallow Stream.
"Have faith," sighed the head gopher. "Let's stay a strong team."
The gophers swung knapsacks over their backs and did up the straps.
They were leaving Pheasant Field forever after the machines' attacks.

Just then, strange thumps and thuds rang through the air.
The throng of gophers all turned at once and stared.
The thousand gopher tunnels had
weakened the earth and mud.

And all Mr Heath's heavy machines
sank to a great depth. **Thud!**

The gophers all laughed at the si_{nki}ng machines
and looked on as Mr Heath arrived on the scene.

Can you complete each word for an item used by the builders, then draw a line to the right picture?

s___ ___d

sho___ ___l

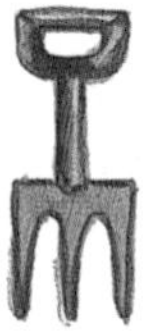

d___g___e r

b___lldo___er

la___ ___er

c___me___t

b___ic___s

___o___k

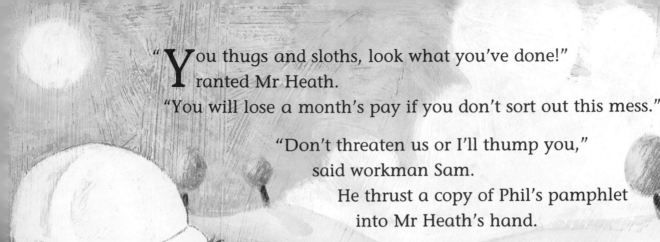

"You thugs and sloths, look what you've done!"
ranted Mr Heath.
"You will lose a month's pay if you don't sort out this mess."

"Don't threaten us or I'll thump you,"
said workman Sam.
He thrust a copy of Phil's pamphlet
into Mr Heath's hand.

"When the phantom gopher rises,
bad men will fall," read Mr Heath.
Sweat streamed from his head,
and he gnashed his teeth.

"My bad workmen have fallen...
I swear this field is cursed!
I'm too wealthy for this stress,
we will build streets somewhere else."

"Pheasant Field is saved, thanks to Phil," cried Big Bill.

"And thanks to the tunnels that you all dug," replied Phil.

Can you replace each underlined word or phrase with a word from the list with a similar meaning?

returned curse snapped dirty excited near bubble depart walked

It dug <u>close</u> _____ to Phil.

He <u>went back</u> _____ to his burrow.

Phil was <u>thrilled</u> _____ .

The workman <u>strolled</u> _____ off.

Phil <u>photographed</u> _____ the phoney phantom gopher.

Phil watched the other workmen <u>swear</u> _____ .

Some people <u>froth</u> _____ at the mouth when they see gophers.

"Those <u>filthy</u> _____ machines are moving in!"

They were packing their things and getting ready to <u>leave</u> _____ .

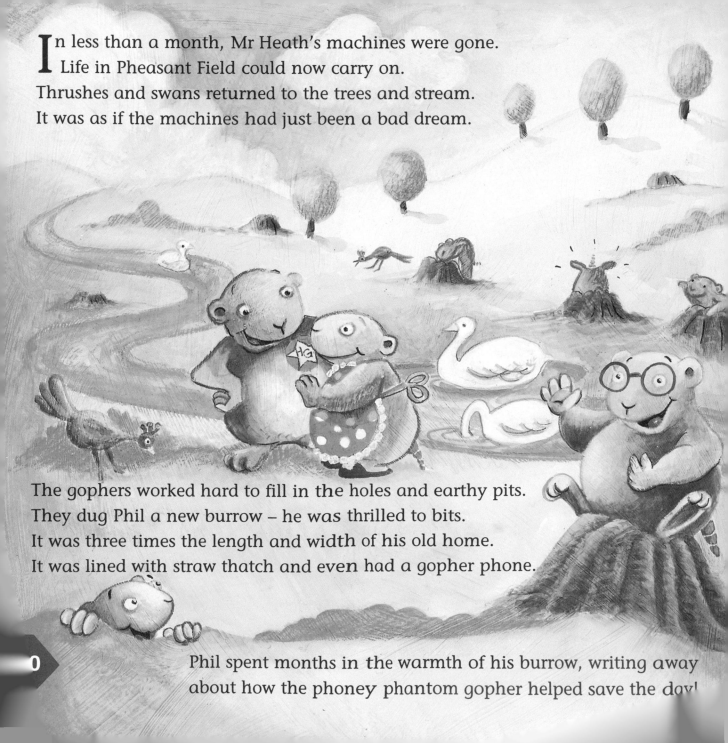

In less than a month, Mr Heath's machines were gone.
Life in Pheasant Field could now carry on.
Thrushes and swans returned to the trees and stream.
It was as if the machines had just been a bad dream.

The gophers worked hard to fill in the holes and earthy pits.
They dug Phil a new burrow – he was thrilled to bits.
It was three times the length and width of his old home.
It was lined with straw thatch and even had a gopher phone.

Phil spent months in the warmth of his burrow, writing away
about how the phoney phantom gopher helped save the day!

Hope you enjoyed the story of the gophers. See if you can answer these questions.

1. Can you name all three of the types of bird that used to live in Pheasant Field? _____

2. Who did Phil tell about his plan for the phantom gopher? _____

3. How many gophers stood on each other's shoulders to make the phoney phantom? _____

4. What was the name of the wealthy man who bought the field? _____

5. What was the name of the head gopher? _____

6. What was the name of the workman whom Phil watched read his pamphlet? _____

7. What part of the field was Phil's old burrow underneath? _____

8. What food did the other gophers feed Phil? _____

Answers

Page 3

path – bath
pheasant – pleasant
phone – throne
stray – sway
earth – birth
south – mouth
north – forth
teeth – beneath

Page 5

thick
thief
field
phoney
thirsty
phantom
free
thimble

Page 7

Beware the **phantom** of **Pheasant** Field.
Please **leave** the **field** to the gophers – or else.
There will be **thunder** and **rain** for **three** years.
When the phantom **gopher** rises, bad men
will fall.

Page 9

trash
seat
boot
horn
wings
fort
heath
trip

Page 11

Check your child's answers.

Page 13

C	S	T	O	P
S	W	A	M	P
T	E	E	T	H
R	E	R	F	O
I	T	H	A	T
P	Q	T	G	O

Page 15

swamp
stride
swede
stroke
swoop
swarm
strap, swap
straight

Page 19

close ➜ near
went back ➜ returned
thrilled ➜ excited
strolled ➜ walked
photographed ➜ snapped
swear ➜ curse
froth ➜ bubble
filthy ➜ dirty
leave ➜ depart

Page 17

shed

shovel

digger

bulldozer

ladder

cement

bricks

fork

Page 21

1. pheasants, swans and thrushes
2. Theo
3. thirteen
4. Mr Heath
5. Big Bill
6. Seth
7. Thistle Thicket
8. strawberries

Published 2005

Letts Educational, The Chiswick Centre,
414 Chiswick High Road, London W4 5TF
Tel 020 8996 3333   Fax 020 8996 8390
Email mail@lettsed.co.uk
www.letts-education.com

Book Concept, Development and Series Editor:
Helen Jacobs, Publishing Director
Author: Clive Gifford
Book Design: 2idesign Ltd
Illustrations: Janet Samuel, The Bright Agency

Letts Educational Limited is a division of Granada Learning.
Part of Granada plc.

British Library Cataloguing in Publication Data

A CIP record for this book is available from the British Library.

ISBN 1 84315 488 9

Printed in Italy

Colour reproduction by PDQ Digital Media Solutions Ltd, Bungay,
Suffolk NR35 1BY